NAME THAT TEXT TYPE!

WHAT ARE GRAPHIC NOVELS?

Emma Carlson Berne

Lerner Publications Company • Minneapolis

For Mrs. Bishop, my fifth- and sixth-grade
English teacher

Lerner Publications Company
A division of Lerner Publishing Group, Inc.
241 First Avenue North
Minneapolis, MN 55401 USA

For reading levels and more information, look up this title at www.lernerbooks.com.

The Prison-Ship Adventure of James Forten, Revolutionary War Captive; *Going,
Going, Dragon!*; *The Book Bandit: A Mystery with Geometry*; *The Midnight
Adventure of Kate Shelley, Train Rescuer*; *The Hundred-Dollar Robber: A Mystery
with Money*; and *Tricky Coyote Tales* © Lerner Publishing Group, Inc. All rights
reserved. *Little White Duck: A Childhood in China* © 2012 by Andrés Vera Martínez
and Na Liu. All rights reserved.

Main body text set in Avenir LT Pro 15/21. Typeface provided by Linotype AG.

Library of Congress Cataloging-in-Publication Data

Berne, Emma Carlson.
    What are graphic novels? / by Emma Carlson Berne.
        p.   cm. — (Name That Text Type!)
    Includes index.
    ISBN 978–1–4677–3666–4 (lib. bdg. : alk. paper)
    ISBN 978–1–4677–4699–1 (eBook)
    1. Graphic novels—Juvenile literature. 2. Comic books, strips, etc.—Juvenile
literature. I. Title.
    PN6710.B47 2015
    741.5'9—dc23   2013040958

Manufactured in the United States of America
1 – BP – 7/15/14

Contents

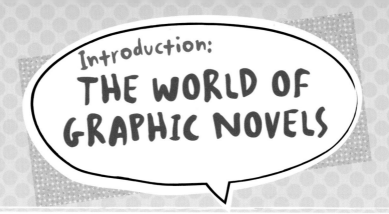

Introduction: THE WORLD OF GRAPHIC NOVELS

You're in a library. You want something new to read. You pull a book from the shelf. You flip it open and gasp. It's a comic book! Boldly drawn pictures fill panels on each page. Speech bubbles float above wild-looking characters. The action keeps you turning page after page.

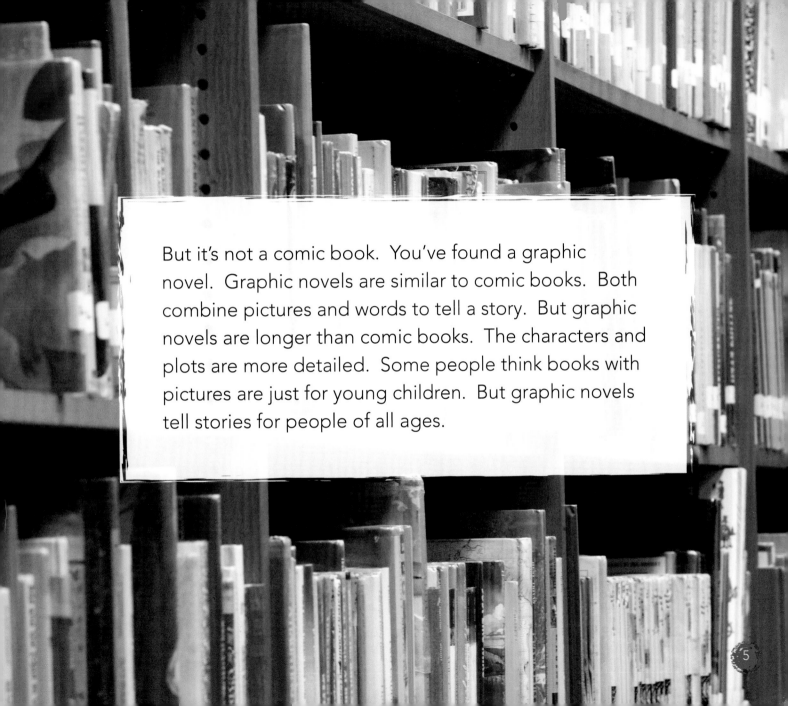

But it's not a comic book. You've found a graphic novel. Graphic novels are similar to comic books. Both combine pictures and words to tell a story. But graphic novels are longer than comic books. The characters and plots are more detailed. Some people think books with pictures are just for young children. But graphic novels tell stories for people of all ages.

Look at the next page. It shows the beginning of *The Prison-Ship Adventure of James Forten, Revolutionary War Captive.* This graphic novel tells about an African American boy trapped on a British ship during the 1700s. When the story opens, the British ship is chasing an American ship, and a fight begins.

NOVELS, COMIC BOOKS, AND GRAPHIC NOVELS

A graphic novel is a mix of a comic book and a novel. A novel tells a story with a beginning, a middle, and an end. A graphic novel does this too. But it uses art to help tell the story. The art looks like comic book art. The characters may look like cartoon drawings. Pages are broken into panels. Each panel shows a picture with some of the story's action. Dialogue is in word bubbles near characters' heads.

This panel comes from a graphic detective novel called *Going, Going, Dragon!* The words in bubbles are what the characters say. The box at the top left tells you the day and the time.

A graphic novel can be as long as a regular novel. A lot can happen in the story. Characters may seem like real people. They usually have lots of feelings. A character may not be all good or all bad. He or she may change or grow during the story.

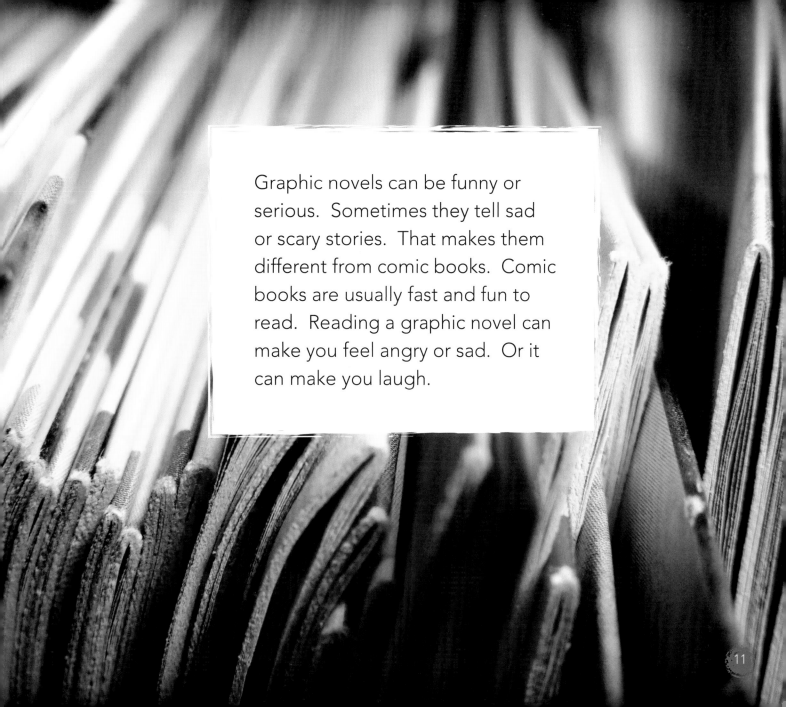

Graphic novels can be funny or serious. Sometimes they tell sad or scary stories. That makes them different from comic books. Comic books are usually fast and fun to read. Reading a graphic novel can make you feel angry or sad. Or it can make you laugh.

ALL SHAPES, ALL SIZES, ALL TYPES

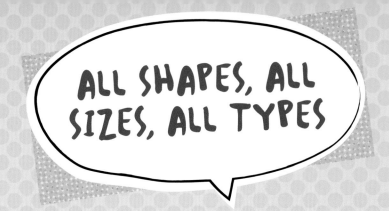

Graphic novels can be about anything. They can take place in the past or in the future. The plot may have spaceships, horse-drawn carriages, or sports cars. Characters can be people or animals. Look at the next page, from the graphic novel *Tricky Coyote Tales*. Two of the story's characters are a bear and a coyote.

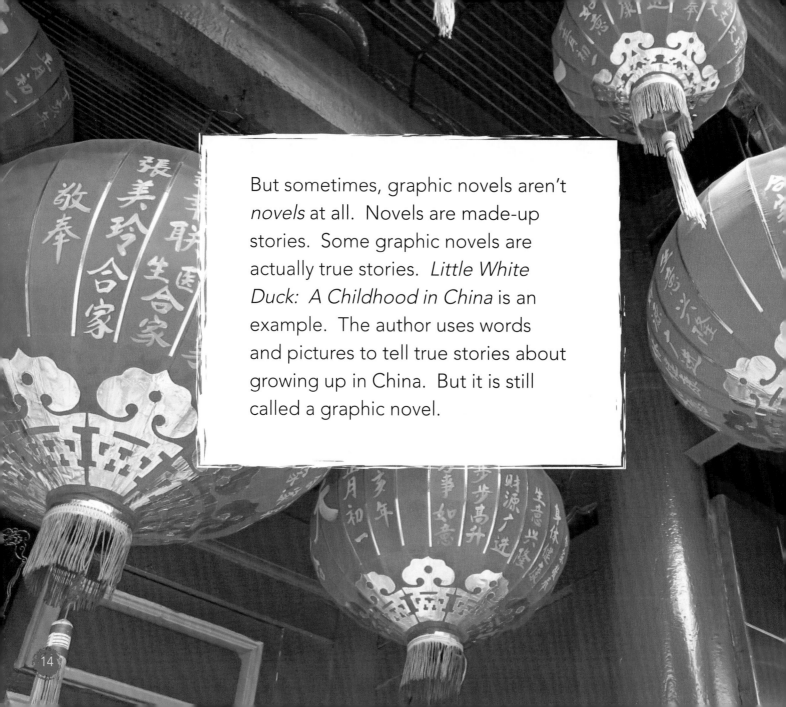

But sometimes, graphic novels aren't *novels* at all. Novels are made-up stories. Some graphic novels are actually true stories. *Little White Duck: A Childhood in China* is an example. The author uses words and pictures to tell true stories about growing up in China. But it is still called a graphic novel.

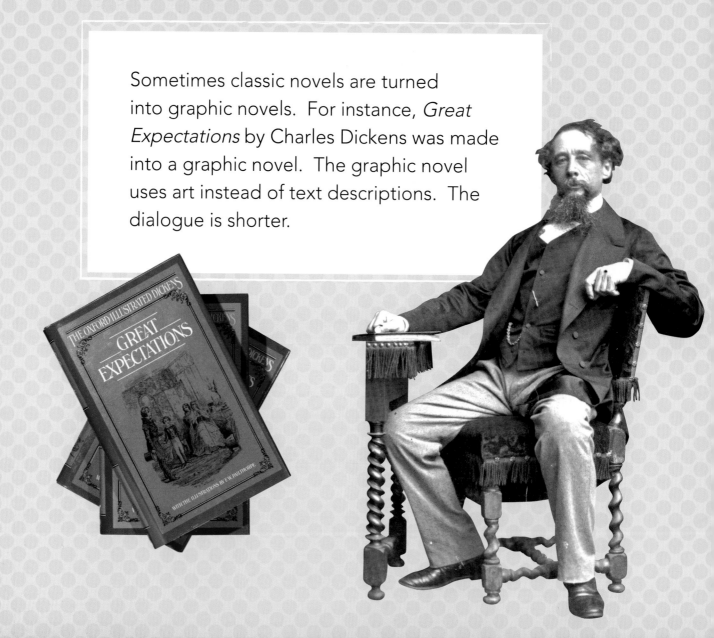

Sometimes classic novels are turned into graphic novels. For instance, *Great Expectations* by Charles Dickens was made into a graphic novel. The graphic novel uses art instead of text descriptions. The dialogue is shorter.

DIFFERENCES IN GRAPHIC NOVELS

Every graphic novel tells a story in its own way. Many graphic novels are drawn like comic books. Characters that look like cartoons are in a made-up setting. The action starts right away. Other graphic novels start more slowly. The art may look very realistic. The action may not start on the first page.

You may see pictures of each character first. Or the author may include old letters or pictures of objects. All of these can tell you more about the story. This page comes from a graphic novel called *The Book Bandit*.

Many graphic novels use dialogue bubbles to show when characters talk. Some graphic novels use no words at all. They tell the story only through pictures.

Graphic novels can show information in other ways too. You may see a journal entry written by a character. In this panel, from *The Hundred-Dollar Robber*, the author uses a notebook to show information.

Manga is a very popular kind of graphic novel. It is published mostly in Japan. The stories can be about anything, from romance to history to sports. Some manga is written just for kids. Other manga is for teenagers or adults.

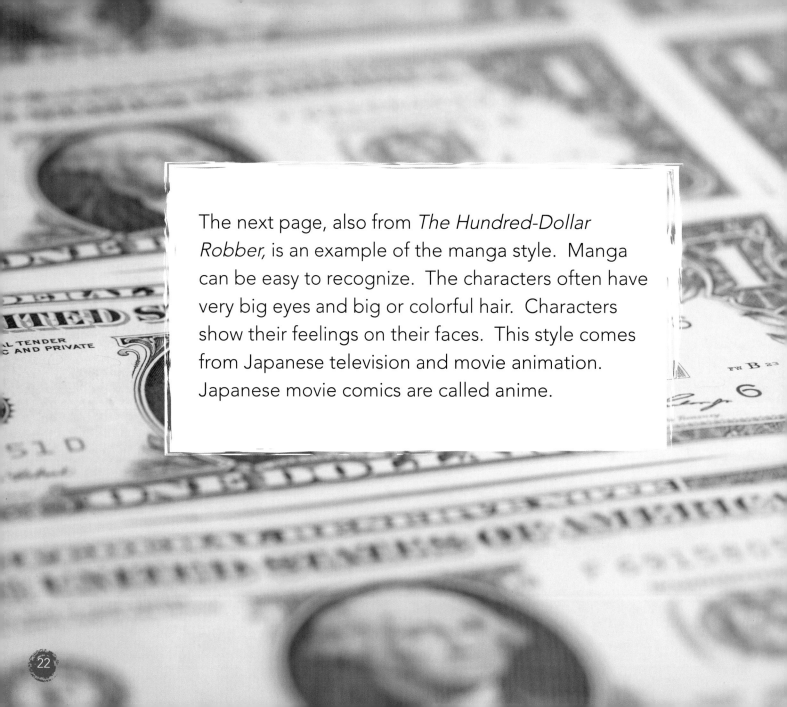

The next page, also from *The Hundred-Dollar Robber,* is an example of the manga style. Manga can be easy to recognize. The characters often have very big eyes and big or colorful hair. Characters show their feelings on their faces. This style comes from Japanese television and movie animation. Japanese movie comics are called anime.

A MAGICAL MASH-UP

Reading a graphic novel can be fun. It can be hard work too. When you read a graphic novel, you take part in the story.

You notice how the action changes from panel to panel. You match the pictures to the dialogue. Do the words match up with the art? You notice changes in the characters' feelings.

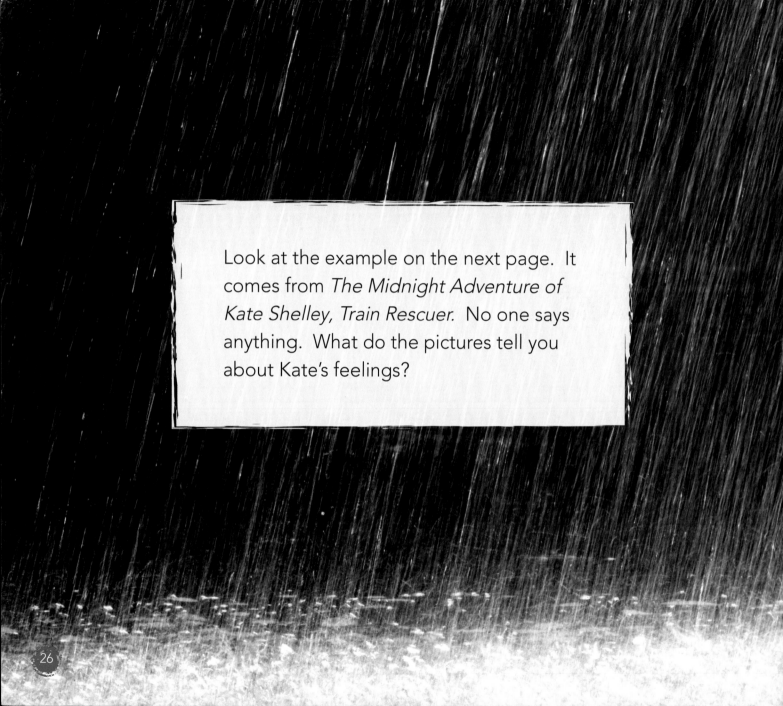

Look at the example on the next page. It comes from *The Midnight Adventure of Kate Shelley, Train Rescuer.* No one says anything. What do the pictures tell you about Kate's feelings?

A graphic novel mixes bits of a novel and bits of a comic book. The author and the artist use these bits to create something new. They may use art and words in surprising ways. You can find all sorts of graphic novels to explore. Pick up a graphic novel and enjoy this magical mash-up between pictures and words.

Now You Do It

Making your own graphic novel can be fun. And you'll have an excuse to doodle in class! Picture your characters in your head. What are their names? Do they like or dislike one another? Where does each one live? Write down everything you can think of about these characters. Then create some drawings of each character.

Next, create a plot for your characters. Do they argue? Are they solving a problem? Can a third character help them? Write down the story you imagine. Then draw some blank panels. In each panel, draw one scene from the story. Draw dialogue bubbles. Have the characters talk to one another. Use the story you wrote as a map to guide you.

Glossary

character: a person or animal in a story

classic: very good and usually very famous

dialogue: words that characters speak to one another

graphic novel: a book that uses cartoonlike pictures and words to tell a story

manga: a style of Japanese comic in which characters have big eyes and show their feelings

novel: a made-up book

panel: a box that holds a picture in a comic strip or a graphic novel

plot: what happens in a story

publish: to print a story and make it into a book

Further Information

The Comic Creator
http://www.readwritethink.org/files/resources/interactives/comic
Use this site to draw and write your own comics online!

Ilya-San and Yahya El-Droubie. *Manga Drawing Kit: Techniques, Tools, and Projects for Mastering the Art of Manga.* San Diego: Thunder Bay Press, 2005. This kit has everything you need to start drawing manga at home.

Marvel Kids: Create Your Own Comic
http://marvelkids.marvel.com/games/play/75/create_your_own_comic
Choose panels and characters to build your own comic strip or comic book online.

Venable, Colleen AF. *Hamster and Cheese.* Minneapolis: Graphic Universe, 2010. Detective Sasspants is on the case of a sandwich thief in the pet shop in this first book of the graphic detective series Guinea PIG, Pet Shop Private Eye.

Whitten, Samantha. *How to Draw Manga Chibis & Cute Critters.* Irvine, CA: Walter Foster Publishing, 2012. Follow the step-by-step instructions in this book to learn how to draw your own manga characters.

Expand learning beyond the printed book. Download free, complementary educational resources for this book from our website, www.lernerresource.com.

Index

Photo Acknowledgments

The images in this book are used with the permission of: © RamonYa/Shutterstock.com, pp. 2, 30, 31, 32; © Lerner Publishing Group, pp. 4, 7, 9, 10, 15, 18, 20, 23, 24, 27 ; © Comstock/Stockbyte/Thinkstock, p. 5; © Kostov/Shutterstock.com, p. 6; © Ryan DeBerardinis/Shutterstock.com, p. 8; © Stockbyte/Thinkstock, p. 10; © Joseph Yarrow/iStock/Thinkstock, p. 11; © iStockphoto.com/kgtoh, p. 14; © DWD-Media/Alamy, p. 16 (books); © John and Charles Watkins/Getty Images, p. 16 (Charles Dickens); © KennyK/Shutterstock.com, p. 17; © mhatzapa/Shutterstock.com, p. 19; © Cityscape/Amana Images/Thinkstock, p. 21; © iStockphoto.com/Steve Debenport, p. 22; © Sami Sarkis/Photographer's Choice/Getty Images, p. 25; © iStockphoto.com/jimkruger, p. 26; © Luis Molinero/Shutterstock.com, p. 28, © Photoraidz/Shutterstock.com, p. 29.

Front Cover: © Lerner Publishing Group, Inc. (book spreads); © robert_s/Shutterstock.com (iPad).